Wild Predators!

Deadly Insects

Heinemann Library
Chicago, Illinois

Andrew Solway

Design: David Poole and Calcium
Illustrations: Geoff Ward
Picture Research: Maria Joannou and Catherine
  Bevan
Production: Camilla Smith

Originated by Ambassador Litho Ltd.
Printed and bound in China by
South China Printing Company.

09 08 07 06 05
10 9 8 7 6 5 4 3 2 1

**Library of Congress Cataloging-in-
Publication Data**
Solway, Andrew.
  Deadly insects / Andrew Solway.-- 1st ed.
      p. cm. -- (Wild predators)
  Includes bibliographical references and index.
  ISBN 1-4034-6566-5 (hc) -- ISBN 1-4034-
6572-X (pb)
  1. Predatory insects--Juvenile literature. I.
Title. II. Series.
  QL496.S65 2005
  595.715'3--dc22
                                    2004018569

Acknowledgments
The author and publisher are grateful to the
following for permission to reproduce copyright
material:
ANT Photo Library p. **40 bottom** (Fredy Mercay);
Ardea pp. **8** (Steve Hopkin), **13** (Eric Lindgren),
21 bottom (Pascal Goetgheluck), **23** (Ken Hoy),
26 (Steve Hopkin), **28** (Pascal Goetgheluck), **31**
(John Cancalosi), **34** (Alan Weaving), **35** (Alan
Weaving), **38** (Ian Beames); Corbis pp. **5 top**
(Neil Miller/Papilio), **5 bottom** (James L Amos),
14 (Anthony Bannister/Gallo Images), **39**
(George D Lepp), **42** (Chris Hellier), **43** (Anthony
Bannister); FLPA pp. **6** (B Borrell Casais), **7
bottom**, **9** (Ian Rose), **12** (Larry West), **21 top**
(Treat Davidson), **25** (Tony Wharton), **30** (Hans
Dieter Brand), **32** (Larry West), **33 top** (Larry
West), **36 top** (Jeremy Early), **36 bottom**
(Winifried Wisniewski), **37** (Fritz Polking), **41** (B
Borrell Casais); Holt Studios p. **33 bottom**;
NHPA pp. **7 top** (Stephen Dalton), **11** (Stephen
Dalton), **16** (Stephen Dalton), **18** (Simon Colmer),
24 (Stephen Dalton), **29** (James Carmichael Jr);
Oxford Scientific Films pp. **10** (Roland Mayr), **15
top** (James H Robson), **17** (Alistair MacEwen),
19 (David M Dennis), **20** (James H Robinson), **22**
(Brian Kenney); Premaphotos Wildlife p. **4**;
Science Photo Library p. **40 top** (Dr Morley
Read).

Cover photograph of a praying mantis
eating prey reproduced with permission of
NHPA/Stephen Dalton.

The publisher would like to thank Michael Bright
of the BBC Natural History Unit for his
assistance in the preparation of this book.

Every effort has been made to contact copyright
holders of any material reproduced in this book.
Any omissions will be rectified in subsequent
printings if notice is given to the publisher.

Contents

Six-Legged Killers

When we think about predators, we often think of animals such as tigers and sharks rather than insects. However, if we were a couple of centimeters tall or smaller, we might think differently! Wherever we lived, from deep in the soil to high in the treetops, there would be insect predators, with weapons such as biting or stabbing jaws, a stinger full of deadly poison, or spiny legs for grabbing.

Insects are the most successful animals on the planet. There are more known species of insects than all of the other animals together.

Cuticle

One key to the insects' success is their cuticle. Insects use it in an amazing variety of ways. Like our bones, cuticle is strong and is used to support the insect's body. Cuticle is also light and waterproof. Thick cuticle is tough, and is used for jaws, claws, and for protective armor. Thin cuticle is flexible, and is used in joints and to line the gut.

Insect relatives

Insects belong to a group of animals called arthropods, along with spiders, crustaceans (crabs, shrimp, and related animals), and myriapods (centipedes and millipedes). All arthropods have a tough outer skeleton to keep their body in shape.

Insects are arthropods with six legs, one pair of antennae, and a body divided into three parts—the head, the thorax, and the abdomen. Many insects also have wings.

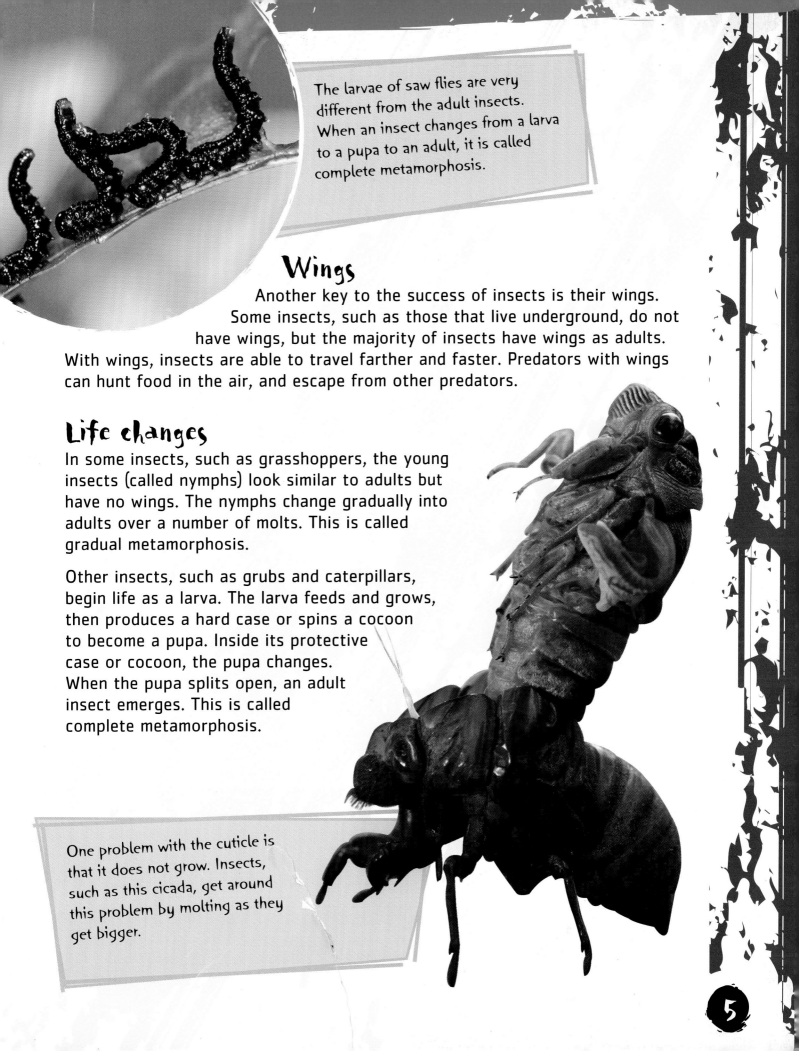

The larvae of saw flies are very different from the adult insects. When an insect changes from a larva to a pupa to an adult, it is called complete metamorphosis.

Wings

Another key to the success of insects is their wings. Some insects, such as those that live underground, do not have wings, but the majority of insects have wings as adults. With wings, insects are able to travel farther and faster. Predators with wings can hunt food in the air, and escape from other predators.

Life changes

In some insects, such as grasshoppers, the young insects (called nymphs) look similar to adults but have no wings. The nymphs change gradually into adults over a number of molts. This is called gradual metamorphosis.

Other insects, such as grubs and caterpillars, begin life as a larva. The larva feeds and grows, then produces a hard case or spins a cocoon to become a pupa. Inside its protective case or cocoon, the pupa changes. When the pupa splits open, an adult insect emerges. This is called complete metamorphosis.

One problem with the cuticle is that it does not grow. Insects, such as this cicada, get around this problem by molting as they get bigger.

Dragonflies

It is a summer evening near a pond in southern England. As the sun sets, clouds of midges gather like smoke over the water. Darting through the midge clouds comes a much larger flier, flicking from side to side as it snaps up its prey. A stray sunbeam across the water catches the dragonfly in flight, lighting it up like a jewel.

The dragonfly family is made up of two groups, the dragonflies and the damselflies. True dragonflies are large, brightly colored, fast-flying insects with two pairs of wings. The front wings are slightly smaller than the hind (back) ones, and while resting the dragonfly holds them out horizontally. Damselflies are slimmer than dragonflies. Their front and rear wings are the same, and they hold their wings vertically when resting. True dragonflies and damselflies are both fierce predators.

Underwater larvae

Dragonflies lay their eggs in water, and the larvae are underwater predators. Dragonfly larvae have structures like a fish's gills that allow them to breathe underwater. The larvae are not fussy eaters —they will eat any animal they can catch. Their prey includes tadpoles, small fish, and even other dragonfly larvae. Some larvae stalk their prey, while others wait for prey to come to them.

Unlike other insects, which either beat both pairs of wings together or use only one pair for flying, dragonflies can beat their front and back wings independently.

Different dragonfly larvae live in all kinds of watery habitats—rivers, streams, lakes, marshes, and even burrows in damp soil. This *Aeshna* dragonfly larva is eating a stickleback underwater.

All dragonfly larvae catch prey using a structure called a mask. In insects, one section of the mouthparts is called the labium, or lip. In dragonfly larvae this is enlarged to form the mask. While waiting to strike, the larva holds the mask folded back under its head. When a victim approaches close enough, the mask shoots out at incredible speed. On the end of the mask are two curved hooks, which dig into the prey. The larva then pulls the mask back in again.

Growing and changing

Dragonfly larvae change gradually as they grow. They molt ten to twenty times between hatching and becoming adults. Shortly before its final molt, a dragonfly larva stops feeding and climbs out of the water. The last larval skin splits, and an adult dragonfly emerges.

An adult dragonfly is emerging from its last larval skin. Adults usually emerge at night or early in the morning, to avoid birds and other predators.

Giant fossils

Scientists have found fossils from about 300 million years ago of insects similar to modern dragonflies. One kind, called *Meganeura*, had a wingspan of 30 inches (75 centimeters)—about the width of an open newspaper.

Not quite adults

Newly emerged dragonflies are not fully adult because they are not yet able to mate. For a short time—anywhere from a day to a month—they leave the water and fly inland to feed and mature. During this time they also develop their bright adult colors.

Darters, skimmers, and hawkers

Adult dragonflies are successful predators because they are superb fliers and have excellent eyesight. True dragonflies can fly backward, hover, and loop, and many species are fast fliers. It is not unusual for the larger species to reach speeds of 19 miles (30 kilometers) per hour. Damselflies are not quite such strong fliers.

All dragonflies catch their prey while flying, but they do not all hunt the same way. Most damselflies and some dragonflies, such as darters and skimmers, hunt from a perch. They sit on a lookout post and dart out on short flights when they spot prey. Other dragonflies, such as hawkers, patrol the air looking for prey and rarely land on a perch.

Nearly all dragonflies will eat anything they catch. They often hunt among clouds of midges or other tiny, biting flies in the early evening.

Dragonflies have the largest compound eyes of any insect. In true dragonflies, the eyes may meet in the middle, while in the damselfly (shown here), the eyes are wide apart.

Compound eyes

Dragonflies have very large eyes. As in most other insects, these are compound eyes. This means that each eye is made up of many separate eyelets, with up to 30,000 of them in a single dragonfly eye.

Dragonflies' compound eyes give them excellent all-around vision, and they are very good at spotting movement. Unlike human eyes, insect eyes can see in ultraviolet light.

Mating and laying eggs

When they are ready to mate, many dragonfly males look for an area of water to claim as their territory. They patrol their patch constantly, and chase off other males that try to invade their space. The males that have territories get more chances to mate with females.

After mating, females lay their eggs on or near water. Some dragonflies scatter their eggs on the water surface. Others have an egg-laying tube on the end of their abdomen, which they use to lay eggs inside plant stems. The females of one species of damselfly dive underwater for as long as an hour to lay their eggs.

This female southern hawker dragonfly is laying eggs. In some species of dragonfly the male helps by keeping watch for predators, or actually lifting the female away from the water after laying eggs.

Mantids

In a forest in Costa Rica, a dead leaf hangs from a thin branch. It sways slightly and looks as if it might fall. Just below, a beetle hurries along another branch. As the beetle approaches, the leaf shoots out two long, spiny arms. They grab the beetle and lift it toward the small, triangular head that has now appeared. A South American boxing mantis has claimed another victim.

With their superb camouflage, mantids are probably the insect world's best sit-and-wait predators. There are about 2,000 species of mantids worldwide. They are found in warmer parts of the world, especially in the Tropics. Most mantids are medium to large insects—the biggest are around six inches (fifteen centimeters) long.

Praying for prey

Mantids are often called praying mantises, because they sit with their long front legs folded under their chin as if they are praying.

A mantid's forelegs (front legs) are its main weapons. They are long and covered in spikes, which makes it difficult for prey to escape. A mantid's jaws look small, but they are very strong and can quickly chop up a grasshopper or other large insect.

Mantids have a wide-ranging diet—they will eat whatever prey comes along. Most of their prey are insects or spiders, but some of the largest mantids catch frogs and small birds.

A mantid may remain motionless waiting for prey or it may sway gently, like a twig in the breeze. After a meal, a mantid will clean itself carefully like a cat.

Sharp eyesight

Like dragonflies, mantids rely mainly on their eyesight to spot prey. The top of a mantid's triangular head is taken up by two large compound eyes. When a mantid sees prey approaching, it slowly turns its head to track the prey's movements. A mantid can turn its head more than halfway around. It can keep prey in sight without moving its body.

When the victim moves within range, the mantid shoots out its long front legs with tremendous speed. Mantids are so fast that they can often pluck a fly from the air if it comes within range.

Mantids sometimes hunt hanging from a perch rather than sitting on it.

Insect gladiators

Scientists have recently discovered a new kind of insect in southern Africa that does not fit into any of the known insect groups. The new insects, known as gladiators or heelwalkers, look like stick insects, but they are predators and catch prey with their front legs like mantids. They are called heelwalkers because they do not walk on the very ends of their legs like other insects, but on their heels.

Masters of disguise

One reason why mantids are such successful predators is because they blend in so well with their environment. In some cases this simply involves being a similar color as the habitat. For example, many mantids in tropical forests are green to blend in with the leaves. In some tropical areas, the leaves dry out and turn brown in the dry season. Where this happens, the mantids turn brown in the dry season, too.

Some mantids have far more elaborate disguises than just coloring. There are mantids that look like twigs, and others that look like dead leaves. In some desert areas there are short, rounded mantids that look like pebbles. And some tropical mantids look astonishingly like flowers. When they are young, these mantids can even change their flower color to match the plant they are on.

Camouflage protects a mantid from predators, such as lizards and birds, as well as allows it to surprise its prey.

Insect camouflage

Many insects rely on camouflage, to hide them from enemies. Some use protective coloring. For instance, some moths match perfectly with tree bark or other backgrounds. Other insects, such as leaf and stick insects, actually look like leaves or sticks. Some bugs have large spikes on their backs that look like thorns. As well as providing camouflage, the spikes make the bugs difficult to eat.

Dangerous mates

Mantids spend most of their time alone, and treat anything that moves as possible prey. This makes it difficult for male mantids when they want to mate with a female. Male mantids are smaller than females, and risk being eaten when they get close enough to a female to mate.

In one mantid species, the European praying mantis, females do quite often eat males after mating. However, in most mantid species, the males have ways of persuading the females not to attack. When he wants to mate with a female, the male moves toward her in a slow, wiggling dance. He has to avoid any sudden moves, or he will end up as her lunch!

Eggs and young

Female mantids lay groups of eggs in a protective case. They can produce several batches of eggs after just one mating. In a few species the female guards the egg case until the eggs hatch.

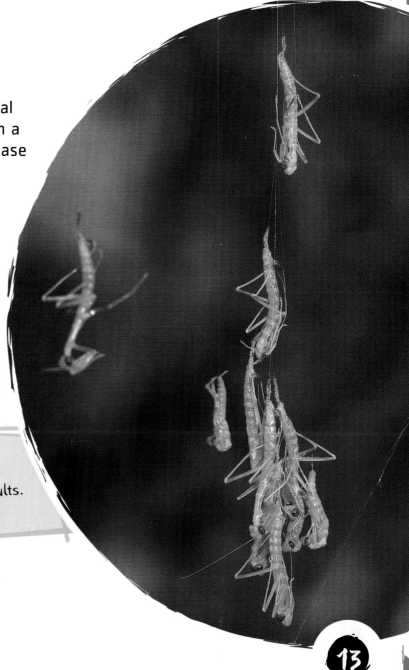

The young mantids that hatch from the eggs look like small, wingless versions of the adults. Within a short time these small mantids are able to hunt for themselves. Many young mantids are eaten by predators before they are fully grown. These predators include other mantids—sometimes even their own brothers and sisters.

These young mantids are molting. Mantids molt six or seven times between hatching and becoming adults.

13

Assassin Bugs

It is early summer in a backyard in Brisbane, Australia. The air is filled with the scent of flowers and the buzzing of honeybees. A honeybee lands on a clump of flowers and begins to drink the nectar. While the bee is drinking, a reddish-brown insect creeps up and suddenly stabs the bee with its long, curved beak.

To most of us a bug is any kind of insect, but to a scientist bugs are a specific order of insects, all of which have long, needle-like mouthparts. Many bugs are plant eaters, but assassin bugs are predators. Most assassin bugs live in tropical areas, but there are a few species in warm or temperate parts of the world.

Liquid food

Some assassin bugs are sit-and-wait predators, but others are more active and stalk their prey. Both kinds have front legs with spines or sticky pads, to grab and hold their prey. They also have a strong, curved beak, which they stab into their victims.

The assassin bug eats by injecting its prey with a mixture of saliva and poison. The poison paralyzes the victim, while the saliva turns the victim's insides into a liquid. The assassin bug then sucks up this liquid, leaving the prey as just a dry husk.

Ways of hunting

Wheel bugs are large assassin bugs that live on shrubs and trees in North America. They prey on caterpillars and other insects. They get their name from a strange, spiky wheel-like part that sticks up behind their head.

There are about 6,500 species of assassin bugs ranging in size from about 0.3 to 1 .5 inches (7 to 40 millimeters). They have a curved beak rather than straight mouthparts.

Like this wheel bug, many assassin bugs have hairs or spikes on their body, to stop them from becoming food for another animal. When danger threatens, they also spray irritating saliva at their attacker.

Most assassin bugs hunt alone, but one kind found in Namibia, Africa, seems to work in groups. These bugs prey on millipedes ten times bigger than themselves. Groups of bugs attack the millipede together. Their combined poison quickly overpowers the millipede, and then the assassins share the feast.

Young assassins

Female assassin bugs usually lay their eggs in cracks or under rocks. In tropical areas the eggs hatch in twenty days or so, but in cooler areas the eggs may take several months to hatch.

Most assassin bugs are predators, but a few species are parasites that live on the blood of other animals. One group of blood suckers are called cone-nose bugs. Most cone-noses are found in Central and South America, and a few species feed on human blood. Their bite is painful, and they can sometimes cause serious disease.

Like dragonflies and mantids, bugs grow by gradual metamorphosis. They take five or six molts to grow into adults.

15

Water Bugs

A female damselfly has been underwater laying her eggs. As she struggles to the surface, four long-bodied insects come scooting across the surface towards her. The damselfly is bigger than them, but she is wet and tired from her long dive. The water striders all stab their needle-like beaks into her body. Within a few seconds their poison does its work, and the damselfly is dead.

Assassin bugs are land predators, but there are other families of bugs that hunt in or on the water. As with assassin bugs, these water-based bugs feed by injecting their prey with a mixture of poison and saliva to paralyze prey and dissolve their insides.

Surface tension

Water striders are able to walk on water because the water surface acts as if it has a very thin skin. This is known as surface tension. It is possible for small, light animals to walk on this skin, if they spread their weight over the surface. A water strider's long legs do this very well. For humans, however, walking on water would be much more difficult. To spread out our weight enough, we would need feet 1.5 miles (2.5 kilometers) long!

This water strider has caught a fly. Like other bugs, water striders develop by gradual metamorphosis.

Water striders

Pond skaters, or water striders, live on the surface of water rather than in it. There are about 500 kinds, ranging in size from from 0.05 to 1.5 inches (1.5 to 36 millimeters). They have long, thin bodies, long legs to spread their weight over the water, and they are covered in tiny water-repellent hairs that help them stay afloat. They move by pushing themselves across the surface with their middle legs, using their back legs to steer.

Water striders live mainly on still water, and feed on insects that fall on the water and get trapped.

Hunting by feel

Water striders have sense organs on their legs that pick up vibrations in the water. When they sense the vibrations of an insect struggling at the surface, they rush to the spot. A water strider uses its short front legs to hold onto its prey while it injects its long mouthparts into its victim's body. Like assassin bugs, water striders suck their victims dry.

Water striders lay their eggs on floating plants or other floating objects. If the water level falls while the eggs are developing, the hatching larvae are not left high and dry. In cold areas water striders survive winter by hiding away in hollow plant stems or other winter retreats. A kind of antifreeze in their blood protects their bodies against ice formation.

Water crickets are closely related to water striders. They are generally smaller than water striders and are short-bodied. This one has caught a wasp.

Back swimmers

Back swimmers, sometimes called water boatmen, are a group of bugs that live just below the water surface rather than on it. As their name suggests, back swimmers swim on their backs. The ends of their long back legs are covered in stiff hairs, making a pair of oar blades. The back swimmer rows through the water with oar-like back legs, and uses its strong front legs for grabbing prey. The back swimmer has large eyes right on the top of its head. Because it swims on its back, it can see forward, backward, and down into the water as it swims along looking for prey.

Like other bug predators, back swimmers inject a mixture of saliva and paralyzing poison into their victims. This means that, despite their small size—no bigger than just over 0.5 inches (17 millimeters) long— back swimmers catch and kill prey as large as young fish. Their poisonous bite is also painful for humans!

Back swimmers are lighter than water, and will float to the surface if they stay still. They have to swim down to stay under the water.

Sea skaters

Insects are successful on land and in fresh water, but very few insects can survive at sea. However, sea skaters, which belong to the water strider family, live on the surface of the sea rather than on fresh water. Sea skaters have been seen feeding on plankton, dead jellyfish, and fish eggs. They lay their eggs on floating objects, such as shells, pieces of wood, and lumps of tar.

Although they live in water, back swimmers have to breathe air. They do this in two ways. They can trap a certain amount of air around long hairs on their body. They also have a long breathing tube on the end of their abdomen, which they can poke above the surface to get a new air supply.

Despite living underwater, adult back swimmers have wings and can fly. This allows them to move on if an area of water dries up or if prey become scarce.

Giant water bugs

Giant water bugs truly are insect giants—the largest species can be almost 4.5 inches (110 millimeters) long. This makes them the largest water-living insects. Like other back swimmers, they swim with their back legs and use their front legs to grab and hold prey while they inject their victims with venom and saliva.

Giant water bugs hunt by stealth, hiding among water plants and ambushing their prey. They eat other water insects, tadpoles, and small fish. Because of their size, a giant water bug's bite is extremely painful to humans.

Giant water bugs can fly and, when they are ready to mate, they fly from pond to pond looking for a partner. At these times they are often attracted to electric lights, like giant moths.

In some species of giant water bugs, the female lays her eggs on the male's back. He then looks after them until they hatch two weeks later.

Lacewings, Ant Lions, and Snakeflies

A small insect with huge, sawtooth jaws wanders through the sandy soil of a French forest. Its tracks look like a child's doodle in the sand. Then there is a change. The insect begins to move slowly inward in a spiral, scooping up sand and throwing it outward as it goes. After about ten minutes, the insect is in the center of the spiral, at the bottom of a steep-sided pit. An ant lion has dug its deadly trap.

Snakeflies, lacewings, ant lions, and their relatives belong to a group of insects called the Neuroptera (nerve-wings). They get this name from the net-like pattern of veins in their wings. The larvae of neuropterans look very different from the adults. They change from larvae to adults by complete metamorphosis.

Lacewings

There are about 5,000 different species of lacewings and their relatives. Green lacewings eat pollen and nectar, but many other types of adult lacewings, and all lacewing larvae, are fierce predators. They hunt aphids, mites, and other plant-eating insects.

Adult lacewings hunt at night, creeping up silently in the dark and then pouncing on their victims. Lacewing larvae hunt by day. Some larvae camouflage themselves by sticking pieces of soil to their bodies. Others cover themselves with the skins of their dead prey, sticking them to spikes on their bodies.

These adult lacewings have ears in their wings! They use them to listen for bats, which are their main enemies.

Singing lacewings

Male green lacewings sing to attract a mate by vibrating their abdomen. This produces a low-pitched sound that vibrates the leaves they are standing on. The vibrations travel to other parts of the plant, and any female that feels them vibrates back. The male keeps up his vibrating song as he goes looking for the female.

Other insects also use sound to attract mates. The loudest singers are cicadas, a kind of plant-eating bug. The chirping song of a cicada can be heard nearly a mile (1.5 kilometers) away!

Ant lions

Ant lions are close relatives of lacewings. Adult ant lions look similar to small dragonflies, but they are much weaker fliers and hunt at night.

Ant lions get their name from their larvae, which are ferocious predators. Some live on tree trunks or burrow into soil. Most live in sandy soil and make traps to catch their prey. To make its trap, an ant lion larva digs a steep-sided pit in the sand. It then buries itself in the sand at the bottom of the pit, leaving only its head and sawtooth jaws sticking out.

An ant lion larva's body is covered in forward-pointing bristles. This means that even large prey cannot pull the ant lion out of the ground once it has grabbed them.

Ant lion adults are similar to dragonflies, but their antennae are longer and have knobs on the end.

Springing the trap

When an ant or other insect comes along, it loses its footing on the soft edge of the trap and falls in. The ant lion larva then grabs the trapped victim using pincer jaws. If the prey tries to climb out of the pit, the ant lion larva picks up sand grains and throws them at the escaping prey. The victim then loses its footing and falls back into the ant lion's jaws.

The larva's curved, pincer-like jaws are hollow. It feeds in a similar way to assassin bugs, injecting saliva to turn the prey's insides into liquid, and then sucking this liquid up.

Some mantispids specialize in hunting spiders—even deadly ones such as black widows! The one in the picture has caught a fly.

Owlflies and mantispids

Two other lacewing relatives that are predators are owlflies and mantispids. Owlfly larvae look similar to ant lions, although they do not dig traps. The adults are much stronger fliers than adult ant lions, and they catch prey in the air. Owlflies can sometimes be mistaken for dragonflies, but they have long antennae whereas dragonfly antennae are short.

Insects in amber

Amber is a hard, transparent, yellow material. It formed from the sticky sap of trees that grew millions of years ago. Many pieces of amber contain fossil insects, including snakeflies. The insects were trapped in the sticky resin millions of years ago and have been preserved in the amber.

Mantispids are similar to small mantids. A mantispid has a long neck, a mobile head, and strong, grasping front legs. Like mantids, they hunt by ambushing their prey. Some mantispids are disguised as social wasps (wasps that live in groups), and hunt the wasps whose appearance they mimic.

Snakeflies

Snakeflies are found everywhere except Australia. The flies get this name because their heads are on a long, snake-like neck. Females look even more snake-like because their body ends in a long, curved egg-laying tube.

Snakeflies are forest insects. Most of them live high in the forest canopy. The main prey of adult snakeflies are aphids and the caterpillars of butterflies and moths. A snakefly runs down its prey, then shoots out its long neck, like a striking snake grabbing its victim.

Female snakeflies use their egg-laying tube to lay eggs under the bark of trees. The larvae live under the tree bark, hunting prey such as young bark beetles. The larvae take about two years to reach full growth. Then they spin silk cocoons and become pupae. After a few days, an adult snakefly emerges from each pupa.

Snakeflies are a fairly small group of insects. There are about 200 known species.

Ladybugs

It is spring in the Sierra Nevada Mountains of California. Everywhere you look, ladybugs are appearing—from tree stumps, from piles of old leaves, and from cracks in rocks. The ladybugs hibernated in autumn last year. Now they are taking to the air in great swarms and heading for farmlands in California's Central Valley. Here they can find plenty of aphids and other tasty prey.

Ladybugs are probably the best known kind of beetles, but there are thousands of others! There are over 300,000 beetle species, which is more than a third of all the animal species in the world. The thing that all beetles have in common is that their front wings are not used for flying. Instead they have become a pair of tough wing cases, which protect the delicate back wings. Most beetles are plant eaters or scavengers, but apart from one small group of plant eaters, all ladybugs are predators.

A ladybug's bright colors are a warning to predators that ladybugs do not make good food. If attacked, they produce a very unpleasant yellow liquid.

Familiar beetles

There are over 5,000 different kinds of ladybugs. The most familiar ones are red, yellow, or orange, with black or white spots. All ladybugs have a very round shape, with short legs and antennae. They are popular with farmers because they eat aphids, fruit flies, mites, and other tiny, plant-sucking insects that damage food crops.

Ladybug adults and larvae both have sharp mandibles for grabbing and chewing their prey. They find prey mainly through scent. Aphids move slowly and are often found in large groups, so they are fairly easy to catch.

Ladybug larvae are gray when they first hatch, but as they grow they develop warning spots.

Like all beetles, ladybugs go through complete metamorphosis as they grow. Female ladybugs lay their eggs on plants where aphids or other suitable prey are found. The larvae that hatch look different from the adults, but they eat the same kinds of prey. The larvae have tremendous appetites and can get through hundreds of aphids in the ten to thirty days it takes them to reach full size.

Larvae molt three or four times, then after a final molt turn into pupae. Between three and twelve days later, an adult ladybug climbs out of the pupa. Adult ladybugs live several weeks or months, depending on where they live and the time of year.

Natural pest killers

Ladybugs are often used by farmers to save their crops from plant pests. For example, farmers growing oranges and lemons in Florida release thousands of ladybugs, known as mealy bug destroyers, in their orchards each year. These ladybugs kill and eat pests called mealy bugs that can damage or destroy the orange and lemon trees.

Tiger Beetles and Ground Beetles

A tiger beetle larva sits with just its head poking out of the soil, watching out for passing prey. The rest of its soft body is hidden below ground. Another beetle walking past comes too close to the larva's hiding place. The larva reaches out and grabs the beetle in its jaws. The beetle struggles and tries to escape, but hooks on the back of the larva's abdomen keep it safely anchored in its tunnel home.

Tiger beetles and ground beetles are closely related, fast-moving predatory beetles. Ground beetles are usually night hunters, but tiger beetles hunt by day.

Tiger beetles

Tiger beetles have large eyes that give them excellent eyesight for spotting prey. Tiger beetles are extremely fast on their feet. Some can move at speeds of over 24 inches (60 centimeters) per second. This may not seem fast, but if the beetle were as big as a human, it would be able to run 165 feet (50 meters) in less than a second.

Tiger beetles are most likely to be seen on sunny days, hunting on open ground. They are fast enough to run down most prey, including other beetles, caterpillars, ants, flies, and grasshoppers.

One way of telling a tiger beetle from a ground beetle is that the large eyes of a tiger beetle make its head wider than its thorax.

Tiger beetles are also excellent fliers. They sometimes make short flights when chasing a victim. Once they catch up with their prey, their large mandibles help them devour it quickly.

Young tigers

Tiger beetles lay their eggs in the soil. When an egg hatches, the larva digs its way to the surface, using its head and thorax like a shovel to carry the soil. The larvae stay in the burrow they have dug for themselves, ambushing and eating passing prey. The larvae enlarge and lengthen their burrow as they grow.

After three molts, the larvae pupate in their burrow. When the adult tiger beetle emerges, it may continue to use the burrow as a place to sleep at night.

A bombardier produces its spray by mixing two chemicals in a special chamber in its abdomen. When the chemicals mix they heat up and shoot out of one end of the chamber.

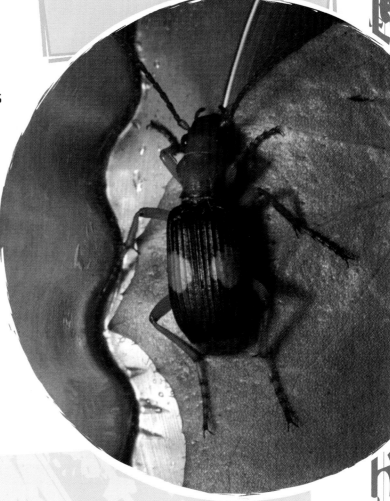

Beetle explosions

Some ground beetles and tiger beetles produce a horrible-smelling liquid if they are attacked, and others can produce chemicals that blister the skin. But one group of ground beetles, the bombardier beetles, have a truly amazing defense mechanism. If a bombardier beetle is under threat, it produces an explosive, burning spray. The spray comes out so fast it makes a popping noise. The bombardier can aim the spray at its attacker using a nozzle on the end of its abdomen, and fire off up to twenty explosive spray charges in quick succession.

Ground beetles

Ground beetles are one of the biggest beetle families. There are at least 40,000 known kinds. The shiny black beetles that scurry away if you turn over a stone or leaves are likely to be ground beetles.

In temperate countries ground beetles are usually shiny black or brown, but in tropical areas they are often brightly colored. In many ground beetles the wing cases are joined together down the middle, and the beetle cannot fly.

Ground beetles are fast movers that actively seek out their prey. Some species hunt any kind of soft-bodied prey, such as slugs, caterpillars, worms, and grubs. Often they hunt at night, using their antennae to follow the trail of chemicals that slugs, for instance, leave behind as they move. Like tiger beetles, their large mandibles help them devour their prey quickly.

These ground beetles have managed to catch a snail to eat.

Specialist eaters

Not all ground beetles eat a range of prey—some are more choosy. Searcher beetles, for instance, eat mainly caterpillars, often going high into trees to find them. In tropical forests, searchers and other ground beetles do not live on the ground at all! They hunt insect prey high in the forest canopy.

Another group of specialists are snail-hunting ground beetles. Some snail hunters have mouthparts like hooks, which they use to pry the snail out of its shell. Others have long, narrow heads that poke right inside the shell. Then they pour saliva onto the snail's soft body to digest it, and suck up the resulting liquid.

Farmers' friends

Like ladybugs, ground beetles help farmers and gardeners by eating pest insects that ruin their plants. Some kinds of ground beetle have been used by farmers to protect their crops from specific pests. The fiery searcher beetle, for instance, was introduced into the United States from Europe because it eats the caterpillars of gypsy moths. Gypsy moths were accidentally introduced to the United States from Europe, and their caterpillars cause serious damage to trees.

Fierce larvae

Ground beetle larvae are also fierce predators. They look like worms, but they have pincer jaws for attacking insects. Many kinds of ground beetles lay their eggs in the soil. The larvae that hatch out live for up to a year below ground, hunting worms, insects, and other soil creatures. They then pupate in the soil. When the adult beetle emerges from the pupas it digs its way to the surface to begin hunting and looking for a mate.

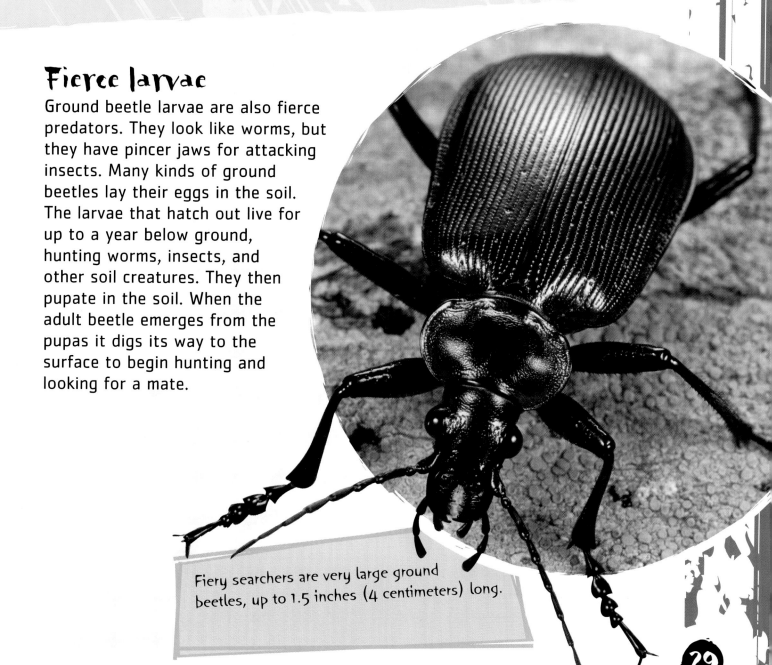

Fiery searchers are very large ground beetles, up to 1.5 inches (4 centimeters) long.

Giant Diving Beetles

At the surface of a shallow stream, a giant diving beetle comes up for air. It lifts the back of its abdomen out of the water for a few moments, then dives again. A space under the beetle's wing covers acts like a diver's oxygen tank, trapping air that the beetle can breathe while it is underwater looking for tadpoles or other juicy prey.

Some beetle species are predators in water rather than on land. There are over 4,000 species of diving beetles around the world. Some can be as small as 0.05 inches (1.5 millimeters), but giant diving beetles are over 1.5 inches (40 millimeters) long.

Hairy oars

Giant diving beetles are fierce predators. They eat water insects, but also snails, tadpoles, frogs, and fish bigger than themselves. They swallow small prey whole, but they tear larger prey to pieces with their strong jaws. Adult giant diving beetles are excellent swimmers. Their bodies are highly streamlined to help them slip easily through the water, while stiff hairs on their back legs act like oars to push them along. They search for prey among water plants.

A diving beetle uses its front legs to grab and hold prey, while its middle legs hold on to underwater plants when resting.

Although diving beetles live in water, they do not have gills and must breathe air. Hairs along the sides of their abdomen help them trap air under their wing cases, allowing them to carry their own air supply.

Even though they spend most of their lives underwater, adult diving beetles can still fly. This allows them to leave a dried up pond, or to leave an area if prey is scarce.

In places with cold winters, diving beetles survive by burying themselves in mud at the bottom of a pool and hibernating. They can slow their bodies down enough to live through the winter buried in the mud.

When a water tiger catches prey, it uses its curved, hollow jaws to inject saliva into the prey and dissolve its insides. The water tiger then sucks up the soupy mixture.

Water tigers

Female diving beetles lay their eggs one at a time in the stems of water plants. The eggs hatch out into larvae called water tigers. A water tiger has a long, S-shaped body with two curved tubes on the end of its abdomen. The curved tubes are breathing tubes. The larva hangs from the water surface with just the tips of its breathing tubes in the air, and waits for prey such as mosquitoes or midge larvae, water fleas, or tadpoles.

When water tigers are fully grown, they crawl on shore and find a damp place where they can pupate. When the adult beetle emerges from the pupa, it returns to the water.

Predatory Flies

A silver weaver spider has begun building a new web. As it spins the web's spokes, a robber fly appears. The fly buzzes around the web, watching the spider. Then it dives in, lands on the spider's back and stabs its mouthparts into the spider's body. The spider hardly has time to struggle before the poison in the fly's mouthparts paralyzes it.

There are about 120,000 known species of true flies. Robber flies are one of several fly families that are predators.

Robber flies

Robber flies are designed for catching prey in flight. They have excellent eyesight and long, bristly legs good for grabbing prey in midair. They use their short, knife-like mouthparts to stab the thorax, or body, of their prey.

Robber flies catch all kinds of prey, including large, dangerous insects such as wasps, bees, dragonflies, and spiders. Most robber flies hunt from a perch. They fly out when they see prey approaching, grab it with their long legs, and stab their mouthparts into the victim's body. The poison that the fly injects stops the victim from struggling, and the saliva dissolves its insides.

Female robber flies lay their eggs in the soil. The larvae that hatch are white and look like worms. They hunt and eat worms and the larvae of other insects they find in the soil.

Robber flies are the biggest of all the true flies. They can be up to three inches (eight centimeters) long. They live in all parts of the world, but prefer dry, open areas and hot weather.

Dance flies

Dance flies look like smaller, slimmer versions of robber flies. Whereas robber flies have short, stabbing mouthparts, dance flies have much longer, slim daggers. There are about 3,000 dance fly species worldwide. They live near rivers, lakes, ponds, and the seashore.

Dance flies hunt in flight in a similar way to robber flies. Dance fly larvae are also predators. Some live in soil or in leaf litter, while other larvae live in water.

Dance flies get their name from the way that males attract females for mating. Groups of males gather over water and fly in a twisting, spiralling dance to attract the attention of females.

Flying aces

Many kinds of insects are called flies, but true flies are a specific group of insects that all have only a single pair of flying wings. The back wings have evolved into two club-shaped structures, called halteres, that help balance. Having only one pair of wings does not make true flies poor flyers—in fact, flies are flying aces. They can turn on a pinhead, hover, fly backward, and even land upside down!

This is a male dance fly. Male dance flies try to attract a female with a gift of a fly or other insect. In some species the male wraps his gift in silky thread spun from glands on his front legs.

Wasps

A mantid stands motionless on a bush, poised to grab prey. A small black-and-red wasp flies by, and the mantid turns its head to watch. The wasp begins to fly rapidly back and forth, just out of reach of the mantid's deadly front legs. After a short time, the mantid seems to lose track of the wasp's movements. Then the wasp darts in and stings three times— once to paralyze the forelegs, and twice more for the rest of the body.

Wasps belong to the order Hymenoptera— the wasps, ants, and bees. About 36,000 hymenopteran species are hunting wasps. Some species live and hunt alone, but other wasps are social and live in large groups.

Some hunting wasps attack large, fierce predators, such as mantids or this wolf spider. They can fly short distances carrying even these large prey.

Powerful weapons

Wasps are among the insect world's most deadly predators. They have strong legs, biting jaws, and they are excellent fliers with sharp senses for finding prey. A wasp's main weapon is its stinger. Its narrow, flexible waist allows a wasp to aim its stinger with great accuracy, even while holding struggling prey.

Nectar eaters

Adult wasps are not actually meat eaters—they live on nectar from flowers. However, female wasps hunt insects or spiders to feed their larvae, which are meat eaters. The females make a nest or burrow, fill it with provisions, and then lay one or more eggs. When the eggs hatch, they have a food supply ready to eat.

Different ways of hunting

The poison in a wasp's stinger can kill its prey, but many wasps only paralyze their victims. This way the prey that the wasps provide for their larvae do not rot before the larvae hatch and eat it.

Many wasps hunt a wide range of prey, but some kinds specialize. Some digger wasps catch only grasshoppers, while others specialize in mantids. Pompilus wasps are spider specialists. There are also weevil hunters, fly hunters, and wasps that hunt cicadas.

Parasitic wasps

Some wasps do not build nests and catch food for their offspring—they are parasites that lay their eggs directly onto or into another animal (the host). When the eggs hatch, they feed on the tissues of their host. At first this has little effect, but as the larvae grow they injure and eventually kill their host. The host may be an insect egg, a caterpillar or other insect larva, an adult insect, or a spider, depending on the kind of parasitic wasp.

Different kinds of wasps build different nests. Some use existing holes or cracks, and some dig tunnels in the ground. Other wasps make nests from daubed mud, like this potter wasp.

Bee wolves

Bee pirates, or bee wolves, are a group of wasps that specialize in hunting bees. They grapple their prey tight with their legs and sting it in the neck. Although the bee may sting back, it can only reach the protected back of the wasp's abdomen, so its stings have no effect.

Bee wolves kill their prey outright rather than paralyzing them. This is because they return to the nest and feed their larvae as they grow, rather than leaving food and abandoning them.

Once a bee wolf has killed its prey, it squeezes the victim to push out all the honey the bee has stored in its crop. The adult licks up the honey, then feeds the corpse of the bee to one of its young.

There are about 1,100 different species of bee wolves and their relatives. While the one in the picture is preying on a honey bee, some species prey on ants and others hunt beetles.

Social wasps

The best known kinds of wasps, such as yellow jackets or common wasps, are social wasps that live together in a large group or colony. A social wasp colony builds a nest containing hundreds or thousands of cells, each one containing an egg or a wasp larva.

Common wasps make their nests from wood, which they chew and mix with saliva to make a kind of tough paper.

A wasp colony is begun by one female wasp—a queen. She builds a small nest and lays a number of eggs that grow into workers, or female wasps that cannot lay eggs. The worker wasps take over the jobs of enlarging the nest, catching food, and feeding new larvae, leaving the queen to lay eggs. The workers feed the larvae on chewed-up prey.

In temperate climates, the wasp colony produces workers through the spring and summer. Then in autumn it begins to raise male wasps and new queens. As winter approaches, the new queens mate, then find sheltered places where they can survive the winter. The rest of the wasp colony dies, leaving the young queens to start again next year.

Killer bees were bred in Brazil by scientists trying to develop an improved type of honey bee. Some bees escaped, and they have gradually spread north to the United States.

Killer bees

Bees are closely related to social wasps, but they feed their larvae on honey rather than on insects. The honey bees that we raise to produce honey have been bred for gentleness, but in parts of the southern United States, a new kind of honey bee has begun to appear. These killer bees are a cross between honey bees and wild African bees. Like other bees they will sting only if they feel threatened, but killer bees are more easily upset than ordinary bees. Although it is very rare for anyone to die from a killer bee attack, an angry swarm can sting a person hundreds of times in just a few seconds.

Hunting Ants

Aquiet forest in Central America suddenly fills with noise—the twittering of ant birds, the buzzing of many flies, and the rustling hiss of countless insects fleeing for their lives. On the ground, a mass of red-black ants, several feet wide, slowly moves forward. As the ants travel, they kill everything in their path. A column of army ants is on the move.

Ants are the most successful predators of the insect world. They eat more prey than any other group of insects. There are over 11,000 different ant species, all of which live in large groups known as colonies.

Wasp and bee relatives

Ants are close relatives of wasps and bees. Some eat leaves or seeds, and some are omnivores, but many ant species are predators.

Many ants have two sets of weapons to attack their prey—biting jaws and a poisonous stinger. Some kinds of ants do not have a stinger, but instead have a different weapon—a spray of acid (burning liquid).

The life of an ant colony

A typical ant colony begins in late summer, when huge numbers of male and female winged ants take flight at about the same time. The female ants are young queens, and they mate in flight with several males. Each queen then lands and rubs off her wings— they will be of no further use, as she will spend the rest of her life underground. She then digs a hole that is the beginning of a new ant nest.

Wood ants live in large nest mounds in cool parts of the Northern Hemisphere. Wood ant queens do not start a new colony alone—they join an existing colony.

38

Ant senses

Some ants have decent eyesight, and all ants can make and hear high-pitched sounds. But ants live mainly in a world of smell and taste. Ants use their antennae or mouthparts to pick up scents in the air or tastes on the ground or on other ants. Members of a particular colony recognize each other by smell. Hunting trails are marked by long-lasting scents, while an ant in trouble will release a fast-acting alarm scent, which soon brings other ants running.

The young queen lays her first batch of eggs, which hatch into worker ants (wingless female ants that do not mate). Some of the workers go out and look for food, while others take over care of the eggs, larvae, and pupae.

The queen continues to lay eggs, and the colony slowly grows. Once the colony reaches a certain size, the workers raise a group of winged males and young queens, ready for the next mating flight.

Ants work together on the tasks of finding food, feeding the young, building a nest, and defending it from enemies. Here one worker gives food it has caught to another ant.

Ant hunters

In the simplest kinds of ant colonies, worker ants go out alone to hunt for prey. Each worker attacks any prey she finds, biting and stinging it. She then carries the food back to the nest.

However, in most ant colonies workers do not hunt by themselves. When they look for food, they usually follow trails laid down on previous hunting trips. As they travel, workers mark the trails with scent. Other workers can then follow their route.

If a worker finds prey, she may simply kill it and carry it back to the nest. However, if the prey is large, or if there are several prey animals, the worker heads back to the nest, laying a new kind of scent trail that tells other workers, "Food this way!" Whenever the worker meets another ant from her nest, she waves her head and touches antennae to tell the other ant about the food. Soon a crowd of ants are heading towards the food source.

This is one of the large soldier ants that guard an army ant colony. Its jaws are so huge that it cannot use them to feed. Soldiers are fed by worker ants in the colony.

Bulldog ants from Australia are examples of ants that are solo hunters. These large, fierce ants will fearlessly attack humans who come too close to their nests.

Ant armies

A few ant species hunt not just in groups, but as a huge mass. Army ants in South America and driver ants in Africa both hunt in this way. Army and driver ants do not live in nests. Instead, they protect their queen, eggs, larvae, and pupae with their own bodies, by forming a huge ball around the queen in some sheltered spot. This is called a bivouac.

Each day, a column of ants heads out from the bivouac, attacking and killing any prey animals in its way. Some ants return with the food, while other ants push the front of the column forward. As it grows, the column begins to branch and spread out. Insects, spiders, worms, snails, and even frogs and chicks are killed and carried back to the bivouac. The ants overwhelm many prey by sheer numbers, but there are also some giant ants guarding the front and sides of the column—up to 500 times bigger than the smallest ants in the colony!

At the end of the day the column retreats for the night, ready to head out in a new direction the next day.

Ant farmers

In some hunting ant species, the workers kill prey to feed the ant larvae, but they themselves live on sugary foods such as nectar. Insects such as aphids produce a sweet, sugary substance known as honeydew. Wood ants keep large herds of aphids and feed on their honeydew. In return for the honeydew, the ants protect the aphids from predators.

A wood ant is herding a group of aphids.

Specialist hunters

Most ants are general predators and will kill any prey that they can catch. However, some species specialize in catching particular prey.

One group of ants, known as dacetines, specialize in catching small, wingless insects called springtails. Springtails can jump away quickly when in danger. To catch them, dacetines have fast-acting mousetrap jaws. These long, thin jaws can be opened right out like a pair of very wide pincers. When a dacetine ant gets close to a springtail, she jerks her head forward, and sensitive trigger hairs on the jaws make them snap shut extremely quickly.

Ants are very strong. They can run carrying prey that weigh more than themselves, and drag much larger prey.

Another ant with strange jaws lives in tropical forests in Central and South America. The jaws have huge spikes on them, like the prongs of a pitchfork. The ant uses these pitchfork jaws to catch a millipede that is covered in long bristles. The ant spears the millipede with her jaws, then uses hairs on the pads of her forefeet to strip the bristles off before eating her prey.

Thieves and slave-takers

Most ant species work hard to build their nests and find food, but a few have found ways of avoiding work. Colonies of thief ants, for instance, live close to colonies of other ants, and steal food from these neighboring ants.

Some ant species go one step further and steal other ants! Large red or black Amazon ants, for instance, raid the nests of wood ants and steal wood ant pupae. The captured wood ants do all the work in the Amazon ant colony.

The end of a colony

Most worker ants live short lives. Some die only two weeks after emerging from the pupa. However, the ant colony itself lasts much longer. Many colonies last as long as the founding queen is alive, which can be fifteen years or more, depending on the species. Soon after she dies, the colony dies, too. However, during the queen's lifetime, the colony will have sent out many young queens to start new colonies.

In a few ant species, colonies do not die with the old queen. For instance, when a wood ant queen mates, she does not start her own nest but goes back to her home nest. The large wood ant nests, which can house over a million ants, have several queens rather than just one. When a colony gets too big, a whole group of workers, plus one or two fertile queens, move out and start a new nest mound nearby.

Most ant colonies have nests underground or in trees. However, some ant plants grow special structures for ants to use as nests. In return, the ants defend the plants from enemies.

Classification Chart

Scientists classify living things (sort them into groups) by comparing their characteristics (their similarities and differences). A species is a group of animals or plants that are all similar and can breed together to produce young. Similar species are organized into a larger group called a genus (plural genera). Similar genera are grouped into families, and so on through bigger and bigger groupings—classes, orders, phyla, and kingdoms.

Insects belong to the class Insecta. There are over a million known insect species in 28 orders. The main insect orders are listed below.

Genus	Number of families	Number of species
Mayflies (Ephemeroptera)	19	2,000
Dragonflies (Odonata)	27	6,000
Cockroaches (Blattodea)	6	3,500
Termites (Isoptera)	7	2,300
Mantids (Mantodea)	8	1,800 to 2,000
Earwigs (Dermaptera)	10	1,900
Stoneflies (Neoptera)	15	2,000
Crickets and grasshoppers (Orthoptera)	39	22,000
Leaf & stick insects (Phasmatodea)	6	2,500
Parasitic lice (Pterygota)	26	3,150
Bugs (Hemiptera)	136	82,000
Lacewings (Neuroptera)	20	5,000
Beetles (Coleoptera)	166	300,000
Fleas (Siphonaptera)	16	1,800
Flies (Diptera)	155	120,000
Caddisflies (Trichoptera)	43	7,000
Butterflies and moths (Lepidoptera)	127	180,000 to 200,000
Wasps, bees, and ants (Hymenoptera)	106	120,000

Insect Body Parts and Life Cycles

Parts of an insect

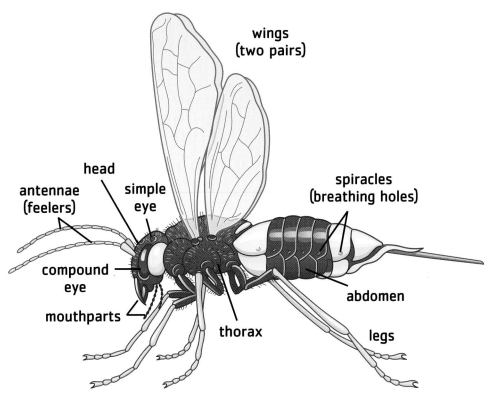

wings
(two pairs)

head

antennae
(feelers)

simple
eye

spiracles
(breathing holes)

compound
eye

mouthparts

thorax

abdomen

legs

Insect life cycles

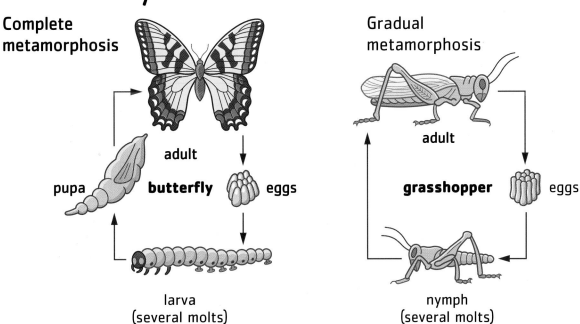

Complete
metamorphosis

Gradual
metamorphosis

adult

pupa

butterfly

eggs

adult

grasshopper

eggs

larva
(several molts)

nymph
(several molts)

Glossary

abdomen back part of the body of a spider or insect

ambush make a surprise attack from hiding

aphid tiny insect that feeds on plant juices

camouflage coloring and markings on an animal that help it blend in with its environment

canopy leafy tops of forest trees

cicada kind of large, stout-bodied bug

class grouping of living things made up of one or more closely related orders

cocoon protective silky case spun by some insect larvae

complete metamorphosis kind of change found in insects such as beetles, butterflies, bees, and wasps, in which the young insect (larva) is very different from the adult. The larva first turns into a pupa, then into an adult.

crop part of the insect gut before the stomach where food is stored

cuticle material that makes up the hard outer shell of an insect

digest break down food so that the body can extract nutrients from it

dissolve mix a solid with a liquid until it becomes part of the liquid

family group of closely related genera of living things

fossil remains of an organism that have been preserved in the earth

genus (plural genera) group of species of living things that are closely related

gradual metamorphosis a kind of change found in insects such as grasshoppers and bugs, in which the young insect changes slowly into an adult as it grows and molts

hibernate go into a deep sleep through the winter

larva (plural larvae) young stage of an insect

leaf litter layer of dead and rotting leaves on the floor of a forest

mandible bone of the lower jaw

mating when a male and a female animal come together to produce young

metamorphosis way that an insect or animal changes as it grows

midge small biting fly often found near water

molt lose a layer of old skin

mouthpart mandible (jaws), palp (lips), or other part of an insect's mouth

nymph young stage of an insect that looks similar to its parents

omnivore animal that eats both animal and plant food

order group of closely related classes of living things

paralyze make unable to move

pincer claw that can pinch

plankton group of tiny animals and plants in the ocean that drift with the currents

predator animal that hunts and eats other animals

prey animal that is hunted and eaten by other animals

pupa (plural pupae) stage in some insects' lives when a larva forms a protective case in which it turns into an adult

pupate form a pupa

scavenger animal that eats dead and rotting meat and other waste material

species group of animals that are similar and can breed together to produce healthy offspring

stalk creep up on something, especially prey

temperate place with a climate that has warm summers and cool winters

thorax middle part of an insect's body

Tropics/tropical land close to the equator where the weather is warm all year

ultraviolet type of high-energy light that humans cannot see

vibration shaking

Further Reading

Boring, Mel. *Take Along Guide: Caterpillars, Bugs, and Butterflies.* Chanhassen, Minn.: NorthWord Press, 1999.

Greenaway, Theresa. *Big Book of Bugs.* New York: DK Publishing, 2000.

Solway, Andrew. *Classifying Living Things: Insects.* Chicago: Heinemann Library, 2003.

Index